Older
Wiser
Sexier

2

OLDER WISER SEXIER FOR WOMEN

This edition © BW Cards Ltd, 2016

First published in 2009

Illustrations by Bev Williams

An Hachette UK Company
www.hachette.co.uk

Summersdale Publishers Ltd
Part of Octopus Publishing Group Limited
Carmelite House
50 Victoria Embankment
LONDON
EC4Y 0DZ
UK

www.summersdale.com

Printed and bound in Poland

ISBN: 978-1-84953-939-5

Older
Wiser
Sexier

Bev Williams

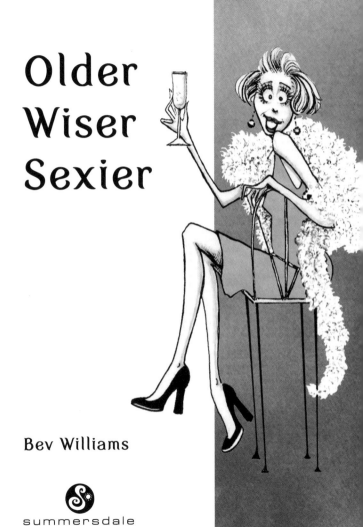

summersdale

Age is just a number. It's totally irrelevant unless, of course, you happen to be a bottle of wine.

Joan Collins

I'm like old wine. They don't bring me out very often, but I'm well preserved.

Rose Fitzgerald Kennedy

'I love cooking with wine.

Occasionally I add food.'

I'm not sixty, 'I'm sexty'.

Dolly Parton

Sex appeal is 50 per cent what
you've got and 50 per cent what
people think you've got.

Sophia Loren

Put a little sparkle
into your relationship
with a little pole –

vaulting.

If they don't have
chocolate in heaven
I'm not going.

Roseanne Barr

Chocolate, coffee, men—

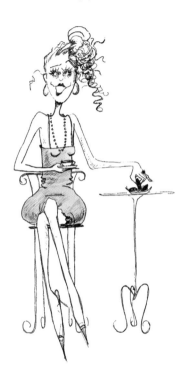

some things are so
much better rich.

I think your whole life
shows in your face, and you
should be proud of that.

Lauren Bacall

Good cheekbones are the
brassiere of old age.

Barbara de Portago

'It's amazing how many of
my stray eyebrows –

are now stuck on my chin!'

It's true, some wines improve with age. But only if the grapes were good in the first place.

Abigail Van Buren

Wine is a living liquid containing no preservatives.

Julia Child

Old age is an excellent time
for outrage. My goal is to say
or do at least one outrageous
thing every week.

Maggie Kuhn

The older one grows, the more
one likes indecency.

Virginia Woolf

At your age, people expect you to be mature, wise and sensible...

disillusion them.

When Sears comes out with a riding vacuum cleaner, then I'll clean the house.

Roseanne Barr

Housework?

Just sweep the room with a glance.

I got my figure back
after giving birth. Sad, I'd hoped
to get somebody else's.

Caroline Quentin

We are always the
same age inside.

Gertrude Stein

'If God had meant me
to touch my toes –

he would have put
chocolates on the floor.'

Beautiful young people are
accidents of nature, but beautiful
old people are works of art.

Eleanor Roosevelt

If you survive long enough, you're
revered – rather like an old building.

Katherine Hepburn

All women over 45 are
really goddesses –

and should be
worshipped daily.

Men don't get cellulite. God
might just be a man.

Rita Rudner

After 30, a body has
a mind of its own.

Bette Midler

One in five men think cellulite is a battery...

God bless them.

I've never met a
woman in my life who would
give up lunch for sex.

Erma Bombeck

Cooking is like love.

It should be indulged in with abandon.

If you obey all the rules,
you miss all the fun.

Katherine Hepburn

The lovely thing about
being forty is that you can
appreciate 25-year-old men more.

Colleen McCullough

'Just how naughty
can we be –

and still go to heaven?'

When I'm old and grey, I want to have a house by the sea. And paint. With a lot of wonderful chums, good music and booze around. And a damn good kitchen to cook in.

You can't turn back the
clock. But you can
wind it up again.

Bonnie Prudden

Fitness – if it came
in a bottle, everybody
would have a great body.

Cher

The best way to enjoy yourself –

is very, very, very badly.

Our ability to delude
ourselves may be an
important survival tool.

Jane Wagner

Time may be a great healer,
but it's a lousy beautician.

Anonymous

'Grey? You call it grey?

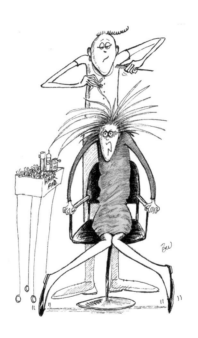

It's stress highlights
– if you don't mind!

I have everything I had 20 years ago, only it's all a little bit lower.

Gypsy Rose Lee

Time is a dressmaker specialising in alterations.

Faith Baldwin

'Mirror, mirror
on the wall...

I am my mother after all.'

Seize the moment. Remember all those women on the *Titanic* who waved off the dessert cart.

Erma Bombeck

My advice if you insist on slimming: eat as much as you like – just don't swallow it.

Harry Secombe

I do wish I could tell you my age but it's impossible. It keeps changing all the time.

Greer Garson

Like many women my age, I am 28 years old.

Mary Schmich

'My husband is quite used to growing old by himself.

I haven't had a birthday for years!'

There comes a time in every
woman's life when the only thing
that helps is a glass of champagne.

Bette Davis

Champagne is the only
wine that leaves a woman
beautiful after drinking it.

Madame De Pompadour

'I'm a multi-tasker.

I go to parties, I smile,
I talk, enjoy great food
and I have little drinkies.'

I worry about scientists discovering that lettuce has been fattening all along.

Erma Bombeck

Birthdays are nature's way of
telling us to eat more cake.

Anonymous

Between two evils, I always pick
the one I never tried before.

Mae West

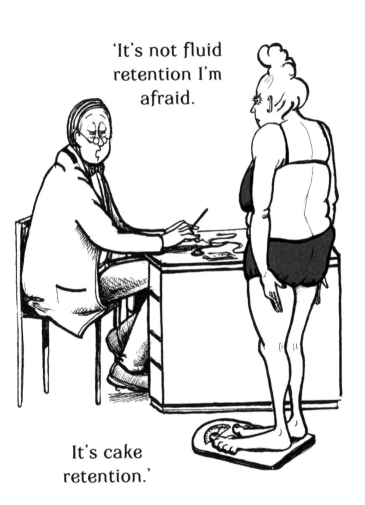

As long as a woman's flesh is clean and healthy what does it matter what shape she is?

Ian Fleming

I would rather be round and jolly than thin and cross.

Ann Widdecombe

'I put on another
pound this morning.

It must be my
new deodorant.'

The best way to get a husband
to do anything is to suggest
he is too old to do it.

Felicity Parker

We learn from experience
that men never learn
from experience.

George Bernard Shaw

When a man appears sexy,
caring and entertaining –

give him a couple
of days and he'll be
back to normal.

One of the best parts of growing older? You can flirt all you like since you've become harmless.

Liz Smith

If I'm feeling really wild, I don't floss before bedtime.

Judith Viorst

'I've sinned

again.'

I never do any television without chocolate. Quite often I write the scripts and I make sure there are chocolate scenes… It's amazing I'm so slim!

Dawn French

Housework can't kill you,
but why take a chance?

Phyllis Diller

As you get older, the pickings get slimmer, but the people don't.

Carrie Fisher

I never worry about diets. The only carrots that interest me are the number you get in a diamond.

Mae West

Life has got to be lived.
That's all there is to it.

Eleanor Roosevelt

The age of a woman doesn't
mean a thing. The best tunes are
played on the oldest fiddles.

Ralph Waldo Emerson

Just take life with a
pinch of salt...

a slice of lime and
two shots of tequila.

If I had my life to live over again, I'd make the same mistakes, only sooner.

Tallulah Bankhead

It's sex, not youth, that's wasted on the young.

Janet Harris

'We only have one regret at our age –

and that's all the sins we didn't commit.'

I have bursts of being a lady,
but it doesn't last long.

Shelley Winters

I mean what's so fulfilling
about fulfilment anyway?

Maureen Lipman

Never go jogging.

It makes the ice in your glass jump.

I believe in loyalty; I think when
a woman reaches an age she
likes she should stick to it.

Eva Gabor

No woman should ever
be quite accurate about her
age. It looks so calculating.

Oscar Wilde

To be an ageless beauty,
all you have to do...

is give up birthdays.
And lie about absolutely
everything.

Time and trouble will tame
an advanced young woman,
but an advanced old
woman is uncontrollable
by any earthly force.

Dorothy L. Sayers

'Take my advice and never drink water.

I've seen what it does to the bottom of boats.'

My doctor told me to do something
that puts me out of breath, so
I've taken up smoking again.

Jo Brand

I don't plan to grow old
gracefully; I plan to have
facelifts until my ears meet.

Rita Rudner

No exercise
is impossible.

Hopeless maybe –
but not impossible.

You only live once, but if you do
it right, once is enough.

Mae West

Good judgement comes from
experience, and often experience
comes from bad judgement.

Rita Mae Brown

On the whole, the years
have been kind to us...

it was just the weekends
that got us into trouble.

The easiest way to diminish
the appearance of wrinkles is
to keep your glasses off when
you look in the mirror.

Joan Rivers

Please don't retouch my
wrinkles. It took me so
long to earn them.

Anna Magnani

Go without a bra –

and pull the wrinkles out of your face.

Old age ain't no place for sissies.

Bette Davis

If life throws you a lemon
– make lemonade.

Joan Collins

'I hear bird flu is now infecting wild creatures and tough old birds.

How are you feeling?'

A woman never
forgets her age – once
she decides what it is.

Stanley Davis

Life's too short to
stuff a mushroom.

Shirley Conran

The secret of staying
young is to live honestly, eat
slowly and lie about your age.

Lucille Ball

Never eat healthy food...

we so need all the
preservatives we can get.

If you're interested in finding out more about our books, find us on Facebook at Summersdale Publishers and follow us on Twitter at @Summersdale.

www.summersdale.com